The Battle of the Somme

Stewart Ross

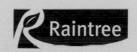

THE WORLD WARS

Copyright Permissions
Raintree
100 N. LaSalle, Ste. 1200
Chicago, IL 60602

Published by Raintree, a division of Reed Elsevier, Inc.

Library of Congress Cataloging-in-Publication Data

Ross, Stewart.
  The Battle of the Somme / Stewart Ross.
    v. cm. -- (The World Wars)
Includes bibliographical references and index.
Contents: The great European war -- Planning for victory: December 1915-February 1916 -- At a steady pace -- July 1, 1916 -- Moving forward -- Attrition -- The Second Battle of the Somme, 1918 -- The legacy of the Somme.
  ISBN 0-7398-5479-8 (lib. bdg. : hardcover)
1. Somme, 1st Battle of the, France, 1916. 2. Somme, 2nd Battle ofthe, France, 1918. [1. Somme, 1st Battle of the, France, 1916. 2. Somme,2nd Battle of the, France, 1918. 3. World War, 1914-1918--Campaigns--France.] I. Title. II. Series.
  D545.S7R67 2003
  940.4'27--dc21

2003000990

Printed in Hong Kong.

Picture acknowledgments
AKG 55; Betty Brown 5; Malcolm Brown 14; Hodder Wayland Picture Library 50; Imperial War Museum 4 (Q87), 7 (Q718), 11 (Q70069), 13 (Q49296), 15 (Q30069), 16 (Q23726), 17 (Q23761), 18 (Q45399), 19 (Q58154), 22 (Q743), 25 (Q3817), 26 (Q23), 28 (Q45556), 29 (Q97508), 30 (Q754), 31 (Q744), 32 (CO874), 33 (Q35445), 34 (Q54), 35 (Q1142), 37 (Q1399), 38 (Q19118), 39 (Q1561), 44 (EAUS572), 47 (Q65389), 49 (Q6850), 51 (Q1568), 54 (EAUS3583), 58 (EAUS166); Stewart Ross 9, 12, 20, 24, 36, 40, 42, 43, 45, 46, 52, 53, 56, 57.
Cover photograph: Imperial War Museum (Q3817). British howitzers during the bombardment that preceded the first Allied attack on the Somme

Contents

CHAPTER ONE:
The Great European War

The Somme River rises near the French town of St. Quentin and flows slowly west through a broad and marshy valley to the English Channel near Abbeville. It takes its name from the unhurried passage of its waters—"Somme" comes from the Celtic word meaning "tranquil." In the latter half of 1916, when enormous armies fought over the land between the Somme and its tributary, the Ancre, a less appropriate name could not have been imagined.

The First Battle of the Somme began on July 1, 1916, and lasted a little over four months. It was, therefore,

July 1916: the first day of the Battle of the Somme. The 2nd Gordon Highlanders approach Mansel Copse during their attack on the village of Mametz.

more a series of actions—a campaign—than one long battle. Nevertheless, whether battle or campaign, the Somme was one of the key engagements of World War I and one of the most momentous in European history.

The European War, 1914

War broke out in Europe in late July 1914. By early August the two sides were clear: France, Russia, and Great Britain (known as the "Entente Powers," or the "Allies") were ranged against the "Central Powers" of Germany and Austria-Hungary. Japan and three smaller states—Serbia, Belgium, and Montenegro—were allied to the Entente Powers. By the end of 1916 they had been joined by Italy (1915), Romania (1916), and Portugal (1916). Turkey joined the Central Powers later in 1914, and Bulgaria joined in 1915.

Lest we forget: This cemetery marks the starting point of the Highlanders' attack, photographed in 2001.

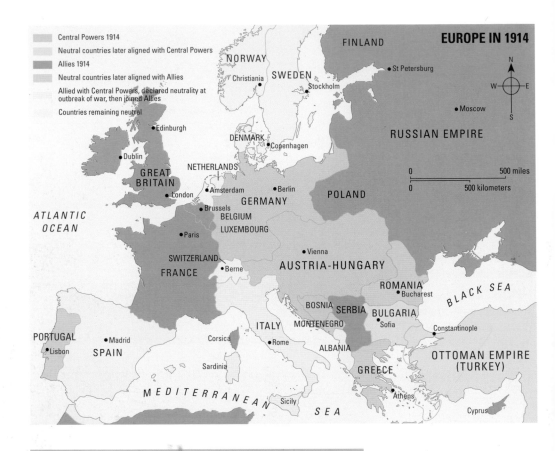

Europe in 1914

Legend:
- Central Powers 1914
- Neutral countries later aligned with Central Powers
- Allies 1914
- Neutral countries later aligned with Allies
- Allied with Central Powers, declared neutrality at outbreak of war, then joined Allies
- Countries remaining neutral

EUROPE IN 1914

FINLAND
NORWAY
• Christiania
SWEDEN
• Stockholm
• St Petersburg
RUSSIAN EMPIRE
• Moscow
• Edinburgh
DENMARK
• Copenhagen
• Dublin
NETHERLANDS
GREAT BRITAIN
• Amsterdam
• London
• Berlin
POLAND
GERMANY
• Brussels
BELGIUM
LUXEMBOURG
ATLANTIC OCEAN
• Paris
SWITZERLAND
• Berne
FRANCE
• Vienna
AUSTRIA-HUNGARY
ROMANIA
• Bucharest
BLACK SEA
BOSNIA
SERBIA
BULGARIA
• Sofia
ITALY
MONTENEGRO
• Rome
ALBANIA
Constantinople
PORTUGAL
• Madrid
Corsica
SPAIN
Sardinia
• Lisbon
GREECE
OTTOMAN EMPIRE (TURKEY)
MEDITERRANEAN
Sicily
SEA
• Athens
Cyprus

0   500 miles
0   500 kilometers

N
W—E
S

The European Empires

The great European powers that fought in World War I were mostly empires rather than countries. Britain and France headed huge empires consisting of territories scattered all over the globe. The German Empire, created in 1871, consisted of the states of Germany (such as Prussia and Bavaria) and overseas territories including German East Africa (now Tanzania). The Russian, Austro-Hungarian, and Turkish (or Ottoman) empires contained regions that are now independent countries, such as the Ukraine (then within the Russian Empire) and Slovakia (then ruled by Austria-Hungary).

A map of Europe in 1914 shows the Central Powers and the Allies, as well as where other nations later placed their allegiance. Countries such as Norway and Sweden chose to remain neutral—that is, not to fight for either side.

Conscripted Armies

The previous century had seen dramatic improvements in technology, communications, administration, and transportation. These developments enabled countries to have larger and more powerful fighting forces than any seen before. At the outbreak of war, almost five million men were ready for military service.

Russia, France, and Germany relied on conscription—required military service for young men—to raise the armies they needed. Britain concentrated instead on building up a hugely powerful navy. In August 1914 it had only 150,000 volunteer soldiers of the British Expeditionary Force (BEF) to send to France's aid.

The Schlieffen Plan

Germany faced enemies in the east (Russia) and the west (France). Accordingly, it planned to move swiftly west, knock out France, then turn all its attention on Russia. The success of this strategy depended on the Schlieffen Plan (first devised in 1905). The plan, which involved attacking northern France through Belgium, almost worked. However, in early September 1914, the French, assisted by the BEF, halted the German advance at the Battle of the Marne.

British soldiers resting on their way to the front line. The sergeant in the foreground is holding one of the most vital pieces of World War I equipment: wire cutters.

Two Battle Fronts

During the fall of 1914 the French and German armies tried to outflank each other, but neither succeeded. As a consequence, by Christmas the front lines of the two sides extended across Western Europe, from neutral Switzerland to the Belgian coast. This was known as the Western Front.

Meanwhile, in Eastern Europe, the Germans had advanced into the Russian Empire. Farther south, the Russians had driven back the Austro-Hungarians. The line of fighting in the east, which was longer and less permanent than the Western Front, was known as the Eastern Front.

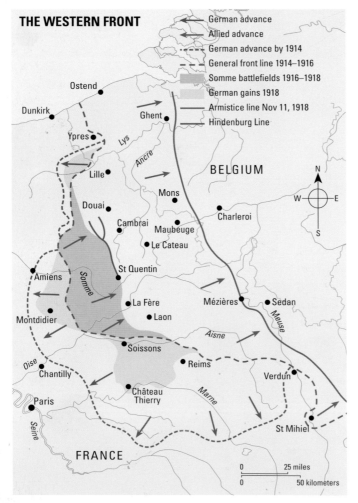

THE WESTERN FRONT

German advance
Allied advance
German advance by 1914
General front line 1914–1916
Somme battlefields 1916–1918
German gains 1918
Armistice line Nov 11, 1918
Hindenburg Line

Ostend
Dunkirk
Ghent
Ypres
Lys
Ancre
Lille
BELGIUM
Mons
Douai
Charleroi
Cambrai
Maubeuge
Le Cateau
St Quentin
Somme
Amiens
La Fère
Mézières
Sedan
Montdidier
Laon
Meuse
Aisne
Soissons
Oise
Reims
Chantilly
Verdun
Château
Thierry
Marne
Paris
St Mihiel
Seine
FRANCE

N / W–E / S

0   25 miles
0   50 kilometers

The Western Front as established by Christmas 1914. Most of the fighting took place in the more northerly sectors, where the land was flatter and more easily crossed.

1915

After five months of fighting, it was clear that the war was going to last much longer than expected. Attacks resulted in enormous casualties but very few gains, particularly on the Western Front. The result was a stalemate.

The situation continued into 1915. In April and May a German attack at the Second Battle of Ypres was repulsed, as was an Anglo-French attack at Artois. In the fall, huge Allied offensives in Champagne and Artois brought further slaughter on a massive scale.

As a result of the failure of these offensives and of the Gallipoli landings (see box), by the end of 1915 the situation on the Western Front was much as it had been the previous January. Both sides were determined that the following year, 1916, would be different.

Defensive Technology

Belief in the possibility of a breakthrough was based more on hope than reality. The cruel truth was that warfare had changed more than most generals realized. Technology dominated, particularly when it came to defense. Two inventions more than any others contributed to the stalemate on the Western Front: barbed wire and the machine gun.

French grenadiers bombing the German trenches on the Somme. Strangely, they have laid barbed wire right across the top of their trench.

Gallipoli

Allied commanders saw Turkey as the weakest link in the Central Powers' alliance. In April 1915, with little sign of progress on the Western Front, an attempt was made to land 75,000 men, many of whom were Australian, at Gallipoli, at the southern end of the entrance to the Black Sea. Their aim was to capture Constantinople and open a southern supply line to Russia. Instead, Turkish forces pinned them to the coast until they were withdrawn in January 1916. In all, some 480,000 Allied troops took part in the Gallipoli campaign, of whom about 250,000 were killed or wounded.

The battle fronts on the Western Front were marked by trenches, usually in lines of three, that sheltered the frontline troops. In front of the trenches stretched roll upon roll of barbed wire. As no man, horse, or wheeled vehicle was capable of crossing the wire, it had either to be cut or blown up. Both tasks were extremely difficult. Even when the wire had been breached, attackers faced devastating machine-gun fire. Weapons such as the German Maschinengewehr, the French Hotchkiss, and the British Vickers could fire between 300 and 600 rounds (bullets) per minute. Each bullet was capable of killing a man.

A cross section of what a typical trench looked like in ideal conditions. In reality, trenches were rarely so neat or so dry.

Faced with a deadly hailstorm of bullets, infantry attacks soon withered. The First Battle of Ypres (October 30–November 24, 1914) had provided an early example of what the new firepower could do. British casualties—many from machine-gun fire—were about 50,000 men. This was the equivalent of one third of the total BEF.

The Allied commanders believed that if only they could get behind the enemy lines, their cavalry would be able to overwhelm all hostile positions from the side. The problem was breaking the front line, which, running from Switzerland to the English Channel, could not be outflanked. Nor were aircraft or airships capable of carrying large numbers of men over it. The only answer was some kind of frontal assault. This had to either exploit a new technology (poison gas had been used in 1915, but to no great effect), or be so enormous that the enemy positions, however strong, would be overwhelmed.

Captain Maurice Mascall of the Royal Garrison Artillery served on the Western Front in December 1914:

"At 2:20 P.M. the bombardment abruptly ceased and the infantry advanced. When they arrived at the edge of the wood they were met by a perfect hail of bullets.... An officer was brought in shot through the lung and another officer was killed just in front of us. This went on till 4:00 P.M. and then it began to get dark.... There was a steady stream of wounded all through the night and it was a horrible sight seeing those poor fellows brought in covered from head to toe with mud."

Quoted in Lyn Macdonald, *1914–1918: Voices and Images of the Great War*

CHAPTER TWO

Planning for Victory: December 1915– February 1916

On December 6, 1915, the leading Allied commanders met at Chantilly, the French military headquarters north of Paris, to discuss their future plans. Most prominent were the French commander in chief Marshal Joseph Joffre and his British counterpart, Field Marshal Sir John French.

In September 1914, when he saved Paris at the Battle of the Marne, Joffre was a French national hero. Even after the costly failures of 1915, his leadership was still largely undisputed. Sir John French was far less secure. The Secretary of State for War, Field Marshal Lord Kitchener, held Sir John responsible for the shortcomings of 1915, and the ambitious commander of the British First Army (the expanded BEF was now divided into two armies), General Douglas Haig , wanted French's job. Two days after the Chantilly Conference opened, French was recalled and Haig took over as commander in chief of the BEF.

France's first commander-in-chief, the resolute but old-fashioned Marshal Joffre, left, rewards one of his men for bravery.

Combined Attack

At first Joffre and Haig could not agree on a common strategy for 1916. Haig suggested the British should attack in Flanders and the French farther south. Joffre wanted a huge Anglo-French offensive, preceded by a series of smaller attacks to wear the enemy down. Haig accepted the idea of one big assault, but questioned the value of the lesser attacks.

The French Army

In the early 19th century, under the leadership of Napoleon Bonaparte, the French Army had been the finest in Europe. Its swift defeat by Prussia (the largest German state) in 1870–1871 was a shattering blow to French pride. Consequently, in 1914 the French Army talked largely of revenge; *À Berlin!* ("To Berlin!") was the battle cry. This emphasis on attack left the army at a serious disadvantage on battlefields dominated by trench warfare.

(Left) General Rawlinson (left), commander of the British Fourth Army on the Somme, and General Haig (right) head for their staff car after planning the Somme offensive.

(Below) Living like rats: French troops take shelter in their dugout.

In the end, on December 29, 1915, the two men agreed that when the ground had dried out there would be a single, enormous Anglo-French offensive. Sixty-five divisions (well over 1 million troops) would be involved in a 43.5-mile (70-kilometer) front. The enemy would be overwhelmed, their lines broken, and, following victory in one heroic battle, the Allies would go on to win the war. The site chosen for this stupendous offensive was at the junction of the British and French armies—on the Somme River.

Allied Optimism

The Allied leaders agreed to commit no further men to "sideshows" such as Gallipoli. Instead, they would concentrate all their resources on the main battle fronts. The Italians would put pressure on Austria-Hungary from the south, and the Russians planned a new offensive in the east. In other words, the Somme campaign would be part of a Europe-wide drive for victory.

The Allies had several reasons to be optimistic about their chances. The entry of Italy into the war in 1915 had brought them 42 fresh divisions (about 840,000 men). By deploying these against Austria-Hungary, they had forced the Austrians to move men away from the Russian Front. Although France's comparatively small population (about 39 million) meant it could not significantly expand its army, it did increase its output of munitions enormously. At the end of 1915, for example, it was producing 1,500 rifles a day. The Russians were better equipped, too. The most significant Allied development, however, was the growth of the British Army.

Kitchener's Men

Of the 150,000 men the BEF had to send to France at the beginning of the war, 90 percent were now casualties. Their places were taken by other regular soldiers—the reserves (210,000 in 1914)—and by the part-time territorial force. This was a volunteer army of 28 divisions established in 1907 to serve alongside regular soldiers in an emergency.

(Right) Welcome to the Army, boys! New recruits are given their uniforms.

(Below) Some of "Kitchener's recruits" line up at Chatham barracks in Kent. They have yet to be provided with uniforms.

When Kitchener was appointed Secretary of State for War in August 1914, he immediately realized that hundreds of thousands more soldiers were required. He called for a new volunteer army of 100,000 men. Before long another 100,000 were called for. Then another, and another, and another. By early 1916 Kitchener had raised six new armies, each of five divisions (a total of some 600,000 men). These men, Kitchener's volunteers of 1914–15, were destined to see their first major engagement on the Somme. To raise still more men, in January 1916 the British government finally introduced conscription.

The "Pals"

One of the devices the British Army used to get young men to join up was to say that "those who joined together would serve together." This meant that those who lived or worked together in civilian life would remain together in the army. Some detachments, such as the Accrington Pals, came from a single town. Others were made up of employees, such as the platoon formed by the clerks of the Cunard shipping line.

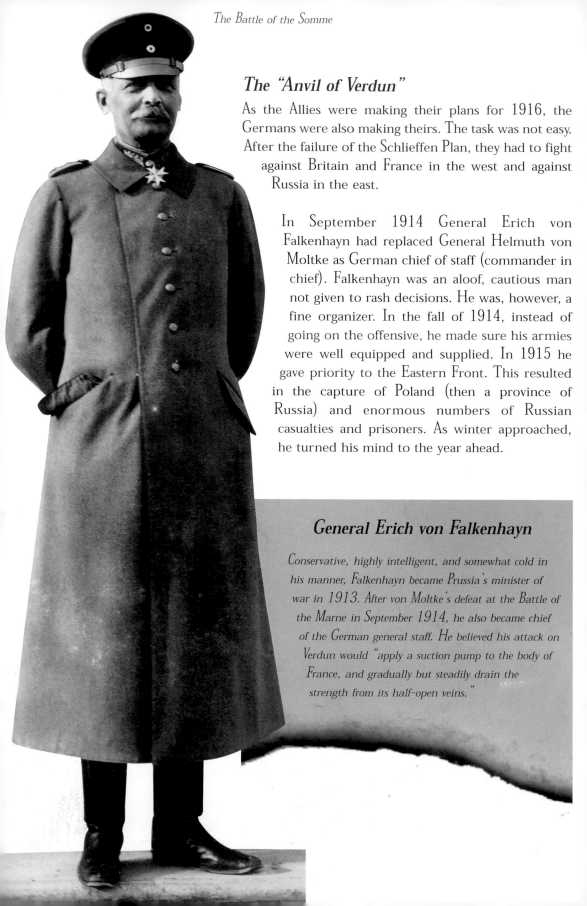

The "Anvil of Verdun"

As the Allies were making their plans for 1916, the Germans were also making theirs. The task was not easy. After the failure of the Schlieffen Plan, they had to fight against Britain and France in the west and against Russia in the east.

In September 1914 General Erich von Falkenhayn had replaced General Helmuth von Moltke as German chief of staff (commander in chief). Falkenhayn was an aloof, cautious man not given to rash decisions. He was, however, a fine organizer. In the fall of 1914, instead of going on the offensive, he made sure his armies were well equipped and supplied. In 1915 he gave priority to the Eastern Front. This resulted in the capture of Poland (then a province of Russia) and enormous numbers of Russian casualties and prisoners. As winter approached, he turned his mind to the year ahead.

General Erich von Falkenhayn

Conservative, highly intelligent, and somewhat cold in his manner, Falkenhayn became Prussia's minister of war in 1913. After von Moltke's defeat at the Battle of the Marne in September 1914, he also became chief of the German general staff. He believed his attack on Verdun would "apply a suction pump to the body of France, and gradually but steadily drain the strength from its half-open veins."

Unlike Joffre and Haig, Falkenhayn did not believe victory would come as a result of one great battle. Instead, he thought it would be a slow, gradual process, wearing the enemy down until their spirit was finally crushed: a war of attrition. He also believed that Germany's major enemy was Great Britain, but Britain could not be defeated until its alliance with France had been broken. He needed a section of the front that would be difficult to defend but that the French, for reasons of national pride, would never willingly abandon. Around the ancient fortress city of Verdun he found such a position and planned to "bleed France white on the anvil of Verdun" with a massive and sustained assault on a narrow part of the front.

The German Army

In August 1914 the Germany Army had 4.3 million trained men. By the middle of the month 1.5 million of them, well equipped with artillery, mortars, machine guns, and grenades, were ready for action on the Western Front. However, the failure to defeat France quickly caused rifts among the German commanders—should they now concentrate on their Eastern or Western Fronts? In 1916 Falkenhayn opted for the latter—hence the attack on Verdun.

German troops marching to the front, 1915. The last few miles were always covered on foot. The men are wearing the new rounded helmets (commonly associated with World War II) that replaced spiked ones early on in World War I.

The German Offensive

On February 21, 1916, following a 21-hour artillery bombardment, 1 million German troops began an assault on Verdun's complex of undermanned defenses. By the third day they had pushed forward 3.4 miles (5.5 km). Joffre's reaction was just as Falkenhayn had anticipated. He put General Philippe Pétain in charge and told him to hold out no matter what the cost. The combined offensive on the Somme was all but forgotten—for the moment.

The hell that was Verdun: craters caused by shelling a railroad embankment, which is no longer recognizable.

On taking command of Verdun, Pétain issued a harsh but simple statement: *Ils ne passeront pas!* ("They shall not pass!"). The titanic struggle around Verdun lasted most of the year. It ended only with a final French counterattack in mid-December 1916. The longest battle of the war so far, it had cost the Germans 434,000 men and the French over 100,000 more. Thereafter men spoke, and only reluctantly, of the "hell of Verdun."

As early as February 27, 1916, Joffre requested that British troops take over a French sector of the Western Front so

Falkenhayn explained to the German Kaiser the thinking behind his attack on Verdun:

"As I have already insisted, the strain on France has already reached breaking point—though it is certainly borne with the most remarkable devotion. If we succeed in opening the eyes of her people to the fact that in a military sense they having nothing more to hope for ... breaking point would be reached and England's sword knocked out of her hand."

Quoted in David Mason, *Verdun*

that French soldiers could be released for the defense of Verdun. By May he was desperate and asked Haig for a British offensive to begin in early July. Haig was alarmed: His new volunteer recruits would not be ready for battle until at least six weeks after that. However, he knew that if he did not act, Verdun might fall. France might then make peace with Germany and the war would be lost. On May 25 Haig wrote to Joffre saying he would attack the German line on the Somme in the beginning of July.

Cheered by a marching band, French soldiers make their way to Verdun. Only fierce national pride prevented the French from being overwhelmed.

Forts

Before the war many experts believed that massive forts of concrete and steel would determine the nature of the conflict. Fine examples of such forts surrounded the Belgian town of Liège. To the surprise of many, the Germans pounded these forts into submission with howitzer artillery guns. However, at Verdun the French held out in forts such as these, defending them to their death and slowing down the German advance. Forts could thus still influence the outcome of a campaign.

CHAPTER THREE

At a Steady Pace

The Somme battlefield was chosen at the Chantilly meeting for the simple reason that it was the meeting point of the British and French Armies—the British to the north and the French to the south. An Anglo-French attack could be launched there with a minimum of logistical difficulty. (Another site could have caused problems with transportation and supply, with each army having to use the other's systems.)

As it turned out, Joffre and Haig could not have chosen a less suitable place to attack. Between the Somme and Ancre Rivers lies a stretch of undulating chalky uplands, known as the Pozières Ridge. The Germans positioned themselves to the southwest of this ridge, allowing themselves to retreat, if necessary, to the higher ground behind. They also looked down on the British to the north of the Ancre.

The Germans had been in position since the first weeks of the war. Between then and the First Battle of the Somme, which began on July 1, 1916, they had turned the line between Maricourt and Gommecourt into the best-defended sector of the entire Western Front.

Private Tom Easton's first impressions of the future Somme battlefield:

"We thought it was lovely country when we got there, because we'd been up in the north before where it was very flat and uninteresting. Here it was all hillier and there were little cottages with gardens and spring flowers coming out. There was a lovely stream nearby and the lads used to bathe in it."

Quoted in Lyn Macdonald, *Somme*

British frontline troops collect their ration of stew carried by hand from the cookhouse behind the lines. After a journey of up to 2 miles (3 kilometers), food rarely arrived hot.

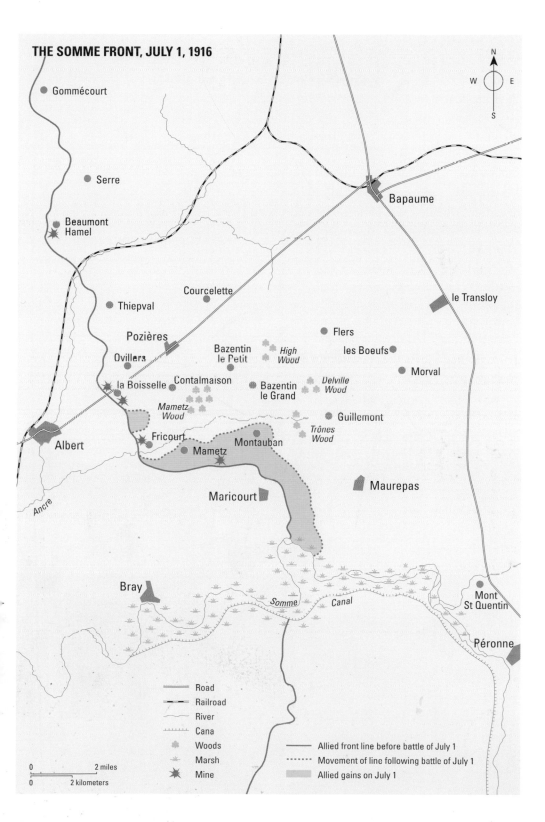

THE SOMME FRONT, JULY 1, 1916

Gommécourt

Serre

Bapaume

Beaumont
Hamel

le Transloy

Courcelette

Thiepval

Flers

Pozières

les Boeufs

High
Wood

Bazentin
le Petit

Ovillers

Morval

Contalmaison

la Boisselle

Delville
Wood

Bazentin
le Grand

Mametz
Wood

Guillemont

Fricourt

Trônes
Wood

Montauban

Albert

Mametz

Maurepas

Maricourt

Ancre

Mont
St Quentin

Bray

Somme   Canal

Péronne

Road
Railroad
River
Cana
Woods
Marsh
Mine

Allied front line before battle of July 1

Movement of line following battle of July 1

Allied gains on July 1

0   2 miles
0   2 kilometers

Almost Impregnable

In many places there were 12 lines of German trenches protected by dense entanglements of barbed wire. Plentiful machine-gun posts covered the lower, treeless ground before them. Beneath the surface, 82 feet (25 meters) into the hard soil, the Germans had dug bunkers that no artillery fire could damage. Sunken telephone wires connected the bunkers and the trenches to command posts in the rear. Six German divisions defended the sector. Most had been there for many months, two of them since September 1914. They knew the place intimately—to a number of them, settled there for more than a year, it was practically a second home. It was against this almost impregnable series of defenses that Haig chose to throw his untested volunteers.

Planning the Somme Offensive

Douglas Haig, the new commander of the British forces in France, was a tough man. Trained as a cavalry officer,

he was somewhat inflexible in his opinions and slow to adopt new ideas. In 1914, for example, he is on record as saying that the machine gun was "a much overrated weapon." Furthermore, Haig seemed to believe that he had some kind of God-given mission to lead his men to victory, whatever the cost. Such confidence can be a great asset to a commander in difficult circumstances. On the other hand, Haig's willingness to make big sacrifices did not bode well for his men.

British volunteers march into position for their first battle

German Bunkers

During 1915 Falkenhayn's main priority on the Western Front had been making the German line secure. Where the soil was suitable for digging (dry and chalky), bunkers lined with concrete (some of it made in Britain) were hollowed out deep beneath the trenches. These bunkers—some holding over one hundred men—were secure refuges during artillery bombardment. As soon as the firing ceased, the men were trained to clamber up the steps and be in position in the trenches within a couple of minutes.

An officer leads a Highland regiment into battle.

Haig had two armies in the Somme area: the Third Army of General "The Bull" Allenby and the Fourth Army of General Henry Rawlinson. Rawlinson was charged with the first assault. Having fought through 1915, he was not optimistic about the possibility of a complete breakthrough. Indeed, unlike his commander in chief, at the Somme he sought only limited objectives. To achieve these, Rawlinson put great faith in the power of artillery to destroy the enemy defenses. This was certainly a practical possibility, given sufficient heavy guns firing at a limited target. However, the British did not have adequate firepower to achieve their objectives, nor did Rawlinson direct his artillery in sufficient density.

Haig stuck to the strategy he and Joffre agreed on at Chantilly: bombardment, attack, breakthrough, and pursuit. He had three cavalry and two infantry divisions at the ready for the final stage of the battle—the pursuit of the enemy. Rawlinson was more cautious. He sought only to capture one line of enemy trenches at a time. This basic disagreement at the highest level about what the army was trying to do did not bode well for the forthcoming attack.

The Fourth Army

When the time for the "Great Push" came, only three French divisions of their Sixth Army could be spared for the Allied attack. They were based south of the Somme River. To the north the British committed twenty divisions, most belonging to Rawlinson's new

Captain R.J. Trousdell described the training his men received in advance of the first Somme offensives:

"The role which each unit was to play on the opening day had been allotted well in advance: training grounds ... were marked out to represent the sectors over which we were to operate, and the attack was rehearsed till everyone knew his part. The actual ground was studied, units being put into the line some days beforehand, and clay models were also made by some units in order to get an idea of the terrain from the enemy's point of view."

Quoted in Lyn Macdonald, *1914–1918: Voices and Images of the Great War*

Fourth Army. Four of Rawlinson's divisions were based on old formations of the BEF, although very few of the original men had survived. Another four divisions were from the British Territorial force, and had been in France since early 1915. A further twelve divisions were made up of recent volunteers.

The volunteers of the Fourth Army had never been in battle before. This applied not just to the infantry, who would have to cross no-man's-land to reach the enemy's lines, but also to the artillery supporting them. This was of crucial importance. Success depended more upon accurate and effective firing from the artillery than upon the infantry's bravery and discipline. There was no guarantee that the newly trained artillery and their hastily manufactured munitions would be up to the task.

Inexperienced though the infantry might have been, they lacked neither enthusiasm nor confidence. They were patriots who had joined up because they believed in their country's cause. They were, they thought, fighting for right and justice against tyranny and evil. There had been plenty of propaganda about German crimes to back up these beliefs. Kitchener's volunteers—the ex-clerks, shopkeepers, gardeners, factory workers, and so on—also had faith in their commanders. At school they had learned about the triumphs of such heroes as King Henry V and the Duke of Wellington. Education and experience had taught them that their political leaders might be untrustworthy, but never their military commanders. The battle would be tough, but they believed that victory was assured.

British short-barreled howitzers fire during the bombardment preceding the attack on the Somme. Many of the hastily made shells failed to explode.

The Role of the Artillery

Before the assault began, the heaviest guns were to concentrate on knocking out the enemy artillery. Since German guns were situated far behind the front lines, fire had to be directed by aircraft or balloon.

Smaller guns would then attempt to obliterate the German front line, smashing the barbed wire, destroying the trenches, and leaving the enemy soldiers paralyzed with fear. After such an attack, Rawlinson believed, all his inexperienced infantry would have to do

The view through the British wire, across no-man's-land. The German positions are being shelled before the start of an offensive.

was simply walk across no-man's-land and occupy the ground before them.

The preliminary bombardment began on June 24, 1916, and lasted for a week. The British had 435 heavy artillery pieces firing at the German artillery, and one thousand field guns concentrated on the German front line. It was the heaviest bombardment the world had ever seen: 1.5 million shells were fired, plastering about 33 tons of high explosive over every square mile of the German front. The noise could be heard over 60 miles (100 kilometers) away, and all who heard it agreed that no one could withstand such an onslaught.

Such hasty judgments were wrong. So were those of Haig and Rawlinson. Low clouds and rain had made "spotting" (directing the artillery from the air) impossible or at best inaccurate. In some places the German trenches were smashed to smithereens, but in their concrete bunkers below ground the majority of the German troops sat frightened but unharmed. In addition, an unusually large number of shells, particularly those imported from the United States, had failed to explode due to poor workmanship. Perhaps most significantly of all, the shelling had failed to cut through the barbed wire. When the bombardment ended, much of the wire remained intact and as deadly a barrier as ever.

Lifting the Bombardment

The timing of the bombardment was crucial. If it lifted (stopped) too late, it risked hitting its own men. If it lifted too soon, the enemy troops would have time to clamber out of their bunkers and prepare to face the assault. On the first day of the Somme, the bombardment lifted too soon. A major problem was communications. Based several miles behind the front lines, the artillery could not see what was happening. They depended on messages reaching them from officers at the front or spotters in the air, often via a distant headquarters. Too often such messages were inaccurate or arrived too late.

At a Steady Pace

Rawlinson did not trust his new, inexperienced infantrymen. The classic infantry tactic when coming under attack during an advance was "fire and movement" —one section of troops lying down to give covering fire while another section moved. Rawlinson knew full well what it was like to come under fire from machine guns on the Western Front: utterly terrifying. He was afraid that once his raw recruits had lain down they would be too frightened to get up again and resume the attack. He also believed that the Germans would have been weakened, if not completely wiped out, by the bombardment. Hence, his troops were supplied with equipment to help them take possession of the German trenches. In addition to ammunition and rations, men also carried items such as empty sandbags, shovels, and grenades.

Howitzers

The armies of World War I used two types of artillery: the cannon and the howitzer. Howitzers were short-barreled guns with a shorter range than cannons. Their shells rose high into the air and came down almost vertically. This made them ideal for bombarding trenches and fortifications. One of the most effective howitzers was the German *Minenwerfer* ("mine-thrower," known to the British as a "Minnie"), whose shells were 6.7 inches (170 millimeters) in diameter.

A German howitzer is prepared for action on the Somme.

A British infantry soldier stands equipped with all his gear.

So Rawlinson issued new orders. When the Fourth Army "went over the top" (climbed out of their trenches) at the Somme, they were to walk "at a steady pace" toward the enemy. The move was practiced in training: Long lines of soldiers, two or three deep, walked unhurried and unflustered toward an imaginary foe. Had the artillery barrage cut the German wire and smashed their bunkers, Rawlinson's tactic might have stood a chance. Had the bombardment not lifted early, it still might have worked. As it was, neither of these things happened—and the Fourth Army walked obediently to its destruction.

Freiwilliger Eversmann, a German soldier, recalled the British bombardment on the Somme:

"They went at it left and right with heavy caliber guns and hammered us with shrapnel and light caliber pieces. Only with difficulty and distress have we obtained rations today. Two of my comrades got fatal hits while fetching dinner. One was Drummer Olleersch ... a dear chap—three days back from leave and there he's gone...."

Quoted in Lyn Macdonald, *Somme*

The attack on the Somme was no secret, nor was it intended to be. Since one of its aims was to take pressure off the French at Verdun, the more the Germans' attention could be diverted elsewhere, the better. Nevertheless, the precise time of the attack was supposed to be a surprise. Two errors prevented this. First, the final barrage stopped early, allowing the German infantry and machine gunners to clatter safely up the steps of their bunkers and into position. Second, one of the huge mines (shafts dug beneath the German lines and filled with explosives to destroy the German wire) detonated early and ineffectively. The scar of the explosion, Hawthorn Crater, can still be seen today.

Major H.F. Bidder remembers the mood in the British trenches on the morning of July 1, 1916:

"There was a wonderful air of cheery expectancy over the troops. They were in the highest spirits, and full of confidence. I have never known the same universal feeling of cheerful eagerness."

Quoted in Lyn Macdonald, *1914–1918: Voices and Images of the Great War.*

A large mine is detonated at Hawthorn Ridge, near Beaumont Hamel, just before the attack on July 1.

"Fix bayonets!": The 1st Lancashire Fusiliers prepare to attack. Note the "street name" on the left, one of the ways troops tried to make their trenches less grim.

Zero Hour

At 7:30 A.M. whistles sounded along the Allied line. From Gommecourt in the north to the French sector on the Somme in the south, a distance of about 14.3 miles (23 kilometers), thousands of soldiers climbed up steps cut into the front walls of their trenches and emerged into no-man's-land. In many places smoke was released from canisters in an attempt to hide the attackers from the enemy gunners, but much of it was dispersed by the southwesterly breeze. As they had been trained, the inexperienced British soldiers began walking toward the enemy lines. Many carried 55-pound packs containing the equipment needed for setting up camp in captured enemy territory. With such loads, they could not have run even if they had wanted to.

No-Man's-Land

The ground between the two front lines was known as "no-man's-land." Before their frontline trenches, each side laid thick rolls of barbed wire. The land between, which could be anything from 88 to 219 yards wide, rapidly became a wasteland of shell craters, smashed vegetation, and ruined buildings. Rats thrived on the bodies of those who had fallen there. Occasionally, parties from either side would venture out into no-man's-land at night to spy, mend the wire, or recover injured colleagues.

31

Massacre

In some places the two front lines on the Somme were less than 328 feet (100 meters) apart. Consequently, the German gunners did not have to hold their fire: they simply blazed away when the British soldiers emerged from their trenches. The Germans couldn't miss. In several sectors of the line, especially those manned by fresh volunteers between Gommecourt and Thiepval, it was hardly war at all. It was a massacre.

In the northern sector of the line, British troops made virtually no gains at all on July 1. Going into the attack in the highest of spirits, line after line of young men were methodically cut down by enemy fire. The German machine gun, the Maschinengewehr, fired 300 rounds per minute. Cloth uniforms offered no protection against its bullets. All the gunners had to do was find the range, pull the trigger, swing their gun in a slow arc, and watch its deadly stream of bullets knock the enemy down like targets at a fair.

The British press came up with a bizarre (and false) explanation for the bravery of German machine gunners:

"General von Falkenhayn ... produced a new type of machine-gunner by taking out of prison thousands of able bodied convicts and allowing them to redeem their sentences by desperate service in the field. Some of these men were chained to the machine-guns they had been trained to use."

Quoted in H.W. Wilson and A.A. Hammerton (eds.), *The Great War*

Canadians go over the top on the Somme.

Angel of Death: The German Maschinengewehr 08 water-cooled machine gun was reliable and deadly.

Thousands—perhaps a majority of the casualties—fell even before they had moved beyond their own defensive wire. The fortunate were killed outright, shot through the head or heart. There was no help for those with shattered legs, punctured lungs, or bodies ripped open. Many survived in the rat-infested no-man's-land for days, but eventually died alone in unimaginable agony.

However, not all perished this way. In several places, when it was clear the attack had failed, the Germans stopped firing. Sickened by the killing, they watched in silence as the less badly wounded dragged themselves back to their trenches.

Gains in the South

The Germans had expected the attack around Gommecourt, but not the attack against the slopes of the Pozières Ridge. Here, between Fricourt and Maricourt, the Allies achieved a degree of surprise and met with limited success. French forces, more experienced than the British, broke though the enemy line and advanced about half a mile through the trees the British called "Caterpillar Wood." Farther west, assisted by better gunnery and an effective smokescreen, volunteers from Lancashire, Kent, Essex, Surrey, Bedford, and Norfolk swiftly took the German front line and advanced over .62 miles (1 kilometer) to the village of Montauban. It was not a breakthrough, but at least it was progress.

The Worst Day

In terms of casualties, the first day of the Battle of the Somme was—and still is—the worst in British military history. It took time for the figures to come in, and even then there were inaccuracies. It was soon clear, however, that over half of the 100,000 men who had gone over the top had been either killed or wounded. The dead totaled about 19,000, and the injured another 39,000: that is 58,000 casualties—the population of a medium-sized town—in a single day's fighting.

Captain Arthur Agius recalls a young officer's death during the attack on Gommecourt:

"This young officer jumped out of the trench to try to organize the men, and was promptly killed. Just disappeared in an explosion. The whole of the valley was being swept with machine-gun fire and hammered with shells. We got the men organized as best we could.... So many gone, and we'd never even got past our frontline trench! .... We were simply treading on the dead."

Quoted in Lyn Macdonald, *Somme*

Terrible though these losses were, they were made infinitely more heartbreaking by their concentration. As Kitchener had promised, those who joined together served together. And now they had died together. One of the cruelest examples was the small Lancashire town of Accrington, which had proudly assembled its own brigade. The one thousand young volunteers of the "Accrington Pals" were brothers, cousins, friends, neighbors, and workmates. On that fateful sunny morning in July 1916, 720 of these "pals" went into action against the Serre fortifications south of Gommecourt. By nightfall only 136 were still standing; 584 of their colleagues were dead, wounded, or missing. The town of Accrington, deprived of its finest young men in a few hours, was devastated.

The Tyneside Irish Brigade walk across no-man's-land. In full view of the German machine guns, they suffered heavy casualties.

Such huge losses would have shaken many commanders, but not Haig. He knew he was waging a war that required steadfastness and utter determination. Any sign of weakness, he feared, and morale would drop and the cause be lost. He believed that his troops' action around Serre had been "cowardly."

The 6th Wiltshires attack on July 1. Marked pathways allowed the men to pass through their own wire by precut routes.

Private Ernest Deighton was wounded on the first day, but managed to survive:

"*I were in the first row and the first one I saw were my chum, Clem Cunnington. I don't think we'd gone twenty yards when he got hit straight through the breast. Machine-gun bullets. He went down. I went down. We got it in the same burst. I got it through the shoulder. I hardly noticed it, at the time, I were so wild when I saw that Clem were finished.*"

Source: Lyn Macdonald, *Somme*

On the evening of July 1, Haig reorganized his troops. He gave additional command to the dashing but reckless General Sir Hubert Gough. The next day the British were to hold back in the north but press forward where gains had already been made in the south. The battle would go on.

General Sir Hubert Gough

Like Haig, Hubert Gough, the British Army's youngest senior commander, was a cavalry man. Dashing, impetuous, and heedless of casualties, he was understandably unpopular with his men. At the Somme he commanded the Reserve Army, which became the Fifth Army in October 1916. After overseeing disastrous attacks at Ypres in 1917, he was relieved of his command in 1918 following defeat in the Second Battle of the Somme.

A field dressing station where the wounded were taken after being rescued from the battlefield by stretcher bearers. From here they were transported by ambulance to hospitals farther behind the lines.

CHAPTER FIVE

Moving Forward

After July 1 there were no more attacks on a similar scale. From then on the British and French offensives were more targeted, more careful. Haig was only too aware that if the first day's casualty rate continued for two weeks, he would literally have no soldiers left with which to fight.

A key area of the battlefield after July 1 lay along the perfectly straight Roman road that ran between Albert, behind the Allied line, and Bapaume, in German-held territory. The village of Pozières, which the Germans had turned into a fortress, stood astride the road about 1.9 miles (3 kilometers) from the original British front line. Before it lay the towns of Ovillers and Contalmaison, and to the southeast the large Mametz Woods. The whole area was filled with an intricate network of trenches, dugouts, blockhouses, and machine-gun posts, many connected with underground tunnels.

Falling angel: the badly damaged church of Notre-Dame de Brerbières in Albert.

Sergeant Robert Scott Macfie confessed his anger at the apparent incompetence of his superiors:

"Our attack ... was directed against a certain village which had been attacked before and has been attacked several times since, always without success. Our performance was no exception to the rule: of my company 177 went up—20 were killed, 42 wounded, and about 8 are missing [and presumed dead]. The want of preparation, the vague orders, the ignorance of the objective and geography, the absurd haste, and in general the horrid bungling were scandalous. After two years of war it seems that our higher commanders are still without common sense."

Quoted from Malcolm Brown (ed.), *The Imperial War Museum Book of the First World War*

July 2–12

For ten days after the first day of battle, the Allies kept up their attacks along the southern part of their line. Some gains were made here and there, but at heavy cost. The fighting was particularly bitter around Contalmaison, where the German frontline trench was captured on July 11.

Around Maricourt and Montauban, where the more battle-hardened French forces were operating, the gains of July 1 were consolidated and further advances made. None of the gains were spectacular, but the constant attacks exhausted the German defenders and put pressure on their high command for a change of plan.

Bazentin Ridge

Haig did not care for night attacks. They were too chaotic for his well-ordered cavalry mind. Rawlinson was more realistic. He bargained that a surprise attack under the cover of darkness had more chance of success against well-prepared positions than a daylight advance, and he finally managed to persuade Haig that it was worth a try.

Realizing that the first Allied bombardment had been too spread out, Rawlinson assembled every gun available for his attack on July 13–14 and directed them at a

Father J.B. Marshall, a Roman Catholic chaplain with the British infantry, describes a trip into no-man's-land on the Somme one day in July 1916:

"*I was told there were fellows out in No-Man's-Land—the old 'No-Man's-Land' before the attack of the morning had converted it into our land. There was one man who they did not propose to bring in because he was practically dead. So I determined to get over the parapet to see him. It was a terrible scene of devastation. I looked at in the twilight—a ground churned up with shell holes, littered with broken wire, and a piteous array of dead bodies.*"

Quoted from Malcolm Brown (ed.), *The Imperial War Museum Book of the First World War*

The British Army's explanation for the failure to push ahead after taking High Wood was that the move had been to buy time while new front lines were secured:

"Owing to the brilliant strategy of the British commanding officer at Bazentin-le-Petit, the principal weight of the German counterattacks was misdirected against High Wood, and there worn down to temporary exhaustion, while the new British line was being built up impregnably at the center."

Quoted from H.W. Wilson and A.A. Hammerton (eds.), *The Great War*

The desolation of war: British troops pass through a once-wooded landscape shattered by shellfire.

narrow sector of the front along the Bazentin Ridge behind Contalmaison. Under cover of this nighttime barrage, four divisions moved forward onto open land. As dawn broke, the Germans found themselves staring at an enemy that was almost upon them.

The attack was one of the most successful of the entire Somme campaign. Supported by well-aimed artillery, by July 15 Rawlinson's men had advanced 3.1 miles (5 kilometers). The German second line was overwhelmed. At one point, the strategically important High Wood was captured.

From High Wood—ideal for directing artillery fire—much of the battlefield was visible. From its summit British forces could see the broad French countryside stretching away into the distance behind the German lines. They were as close as they would ever be to a breakthrough. Despite this, the British troops were withdrawn from High Wood on July 16. Their commanders had decided that they had insufficient troops to continue with the attack and that the position was too dangerous to hold, so a rare opportunity was missed.

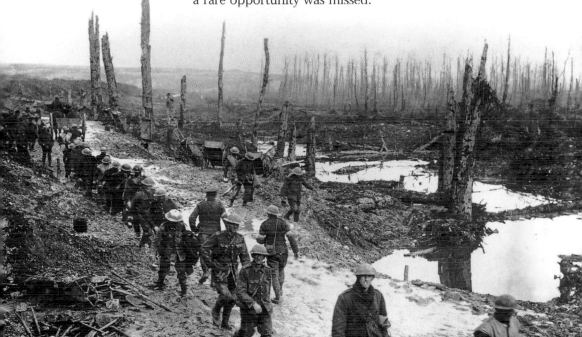

Delville Wood and Pozières

Meanwhile, the battle raged on. Southwest of High Wood the British cavalry saw action for the first time in the war. One of the last cavalry charges in British history brought temporary gains before the horsemen were driven off by machine-gun fire. To the east, the South African Brigade fought a monumental battle to take and then hold Delville Wood. About 3.7 miles (6 kilometers) to the west, on July 23, Australian and New Zealand forces seized the Pozières fortress north of Contalmaison. By the end of July, Haig could take some satisfaction from what had been achieved. There had been no breakthrough, but he was sure the enemy had been rattled.

An Australian gun crew in action on the Somme.

The German Response

Haig was right. On July 1 von Falkenhayn was horrified to hear of plans to abandon his second line of defenses on the left bank of the Somme. He canceled the move and set up a meeting the next day with the army's chief defensive expert, Colonel Fritz von Lossberg (1868–1943). Lossberg had made his name organizing resistance to the Allied attacks of 1915. His strategy, eventually that of the entire German Army, was "mobile defense in depth." Instead of holding a rigid line at all costs, he placed only a few troops at the front and held the bulk back as reserves. From there they could make swift counterattacks where needed.

ANZAC

When war broke out, Australia and New Zealand, both within the British Empire, had no armies of their own. The Australian and New Zealand Army Corps (ANZAC) was formed in 1914. Starting as a force of about 25,000 volunteers, it rose to five divisions (approximately 100,000 men) by 1916. The ANZAC first saw service in Gallipoli and some of these troops went on to France in time for the Battle of the Somme. As the battle dragged on, they played a key role in the offensive.

Lossberg also believed in the strategy of adapting craters made by the enemy artillery instead of digging trenches. Each crater became a mini-fortress able to give covering fire to its neighbors. The result was a sort of deep defensive carpet that was difficult to break through and from which counterattacks were easy. As the Allies soon discovered, the strategy was highly effective.

Falkenhayn asked Lossberg to take command of the defenses on the Somme. Lossberg agreed, as long as the German offensive at Verdun was called off. His mobile defense would not work without sufficient troops in reserve. These men could come only from Verdun. Falkenhayn agreed, and Lossberg took over as the German Second Army's chief of staff. However, Falkenhayn was unwilling to accept that his Verdun plan had failed, and he did not keep his word. By the end of July, Falkenhayn was giving ground at Verdun and on the Somme. He was also having to send troops to help his hard-pressed Austrian allies on the Eastern Front. Not surprisingly, his position as commander in chief was looking increasingly shaky.

The appointment of Lossberg was not the only change that the Somme offensive forced on Falkenhayn. On July 14, as Rawlinson's night attack was hammering a large dent in his line, Falkenhayn reorganized his command.

The Somme front was divided in two. General Otto von Below, who had previously commanded the whole front, was moved to a smaller northern sector. He was placed under the overall command of the experienced artillery officer General Max von Gallwitz, who was now also in charge of a southern sector manned by a new First Army. Meanwhile, the Germans had been pouring reinforcements into the Somme

South Africans

South Africa was part of the British Empire. Between 1899 and 1902 Britain had fought a war there to prevent two of its provinces—Transvaal and Orange Free State—from becoming independent. South Africans loyal to Britain had fought with the British Army. In 1914–1915 they again saw service, this time against German East Africa. When they arrived in Europe they were among Haig's most able and experienced troops.

battlefield. On July 1 they had six divisions manning the line. Two weeks later there were twelve, with more on the way. They were troops the German high command could not afford to spare.

The Bigger Picture

The first and most obvious outcome of the battle so far had been the horrendous British losses on the first day. These were significant for political and social as well as military reasons. During the rest of July 1916, during which 26.1 square miles (42 square kilometers) of enemy territory were captured, the Allied picture was less grim. By July 31, on top of the 58,000 casualties of the first day, the Allies had sustained a further 143,000 casualties. By this time the total German casualties had reached around 166,000. In other words, after their comparatively light losses on July 1, they were now suffering more heavily than the Allies. In addition, Falkenhayn was under growing pressure to withdraw men from Verdun. The new British Army, improving with each day's experience, was now a major factor in the war. Its emergence had shifted the balance of power sharply in the Allies' favor.

By August 1916 the Allied commanders could view the progress of the war with some optimism. The Russian offensive against Austria had gone well. Encouraged by this, Romania was on the verge of joining the Allies. There was no question about it: the Somme offensive had to continue.

From the diary of Guy Chapman, November 16, 1916:

"There is a sickly smell of gas, blood, putrefying corpses, and broken bricks. Here and there lie the bodies of the fallen.... The burial parties work without ceasing, 800 Englishmen and 40 Germans were buried yesterday—evidence of what price the assaulting parties must pay for some few yards of ground."

Quoted from Peter Liddle, *The 1916 Battle of the Somme*

Some of the luckier ones: German prisoners are escorted behind the Allied lines.

CHAPTER SIX:
Attrition

By the end of 1915, the civil and military leaders on both sides were beginning to realize that they were engaged in a war the like of which had never been seen before. It was not a conflict of dashing movement and brilliant victories, but one of endurance, of wearing the enemy down: a war of attrition. Victory would come to the side that could best withstand casualties and maintain morale. After the failures of July 1, this was now the pattern on the Somme.

August 1916 was a difficult month for Douglas Haig. Despite the unprecedented expenditure of money, men, and munitions, it was clear that things were not going according to plan. Officials spoke of "substantial progress" and "grinding the enemy down." By and large the press did its patriotic duty by reporting events in as optimistic a way as possible. Even so, voices of dissent were beginning to be heard.

General Rawlinson explains the Allied position to King George V (left foreground) during his visit to the Somme battlefield. The commander of the 3rd Army Corps, General Congreve, is holding the map.

Dissent

The most influential voice was that of Winston Churchill, the ex-minister who was now serving with the army in France. On August 1 Churchill sent a memorandum to every member of the cabinet in which he concluded of the Somme offensive: "In personnel the results of the operation have been disastrous; in terrain they have been absolutely barren." The British government was alarmed but had little choice but to continue its support of Haig. To dismiss the commander in chief in the middle of an offensive would severely damage morale. Besides, a second change of commander in less than a year would indicate panic.

Part of a memorandum sent by Churchill to the cabinet on August 1, 1916, read:

"We are using up division after division not only those originally concentrated for the attack, but many taken from all parts of the line. After being put through the mill and losing perhaps half their infantry and two-thirds of their infantry officers, these shattered divisions will take several months to recover, especially as they will in many cases have to go into the trenches at once.... Thus the pent-up energies of the army are being [wasted]."

Quoted from Winston Churchill, *World Crisis, 1911–1918*

King George V was pleased by the government's continued support of Haig. In the second week of August the king visited France to see how things were going. To impress the king, Haig orderered an Anglo-French attack around the village of Guillemont. It proved to be yet another failure. Despite this, after receiving as favorable a picture of events as was possible, the king returned home convinced that Haig was doing all that could be done in tough circumstances.

On August 14 Haig encountered another obstacle—the weather. After a succession of dry weeks, the sky opened. Rivers and streams swelled, broken drains and ditches flooded, trenches filled with water, and in many areas no-man's-land became a swamp. Hampered by the conditions, Allied attacks during the second half of August struggled to make any headway.

German Difficulties

If things were bad for the British high command, they were worse for the Germans. France had not been broken by the attack on Verdun. In fact, by August 1916 the French were beginning to claw back some of the territory lost in the first half of the year. Meanwhile, on the Eastern Front, a massive attack had been launched by the Russians in early July on the Austro-German forces in the southern sector of the front. The Russians' rapid gains of the first few weeks were eventually halted, but only after Falkenhayn had been obliged to transfer five of his best divisions to the east. Their inexperienced and under-trained replacements on the Western Front were so hopeless that Falkenhayn rejected them as unfit for frontline service.

Also of key importance—and a novel development in war—was the fact that the Allies had gained control of the air. Air supremacy was vital not just for bombing but also for directing artillery fire and discovering the positions and movements of enemy forces. By the summer of 1916 the German Fokker E-Type aircraft, which had dominated the skies since mid-1915, were

Since trenches were really little more than ditches; in wet weather they filled with filthy water that swiftly churned into mud.

losing their position to the latest French Nieuports and planes of the British Royal Aircraft Factory and Sopwith Company.

The Fall of Falkenhayn

At the end of August 1916 Falkenhayn's position was impossible. His armies were being battered at Verdun and on the Somme, and Romania was on the point of joining the Allies. Only on the Eastern Front, where the Kaiser's forces were commanded by the elderly Field Marshal Paul von Hindenburg and his brilliant chief of staff, Erich Ludendorff, had German victories been recorded.

On August 28 Falkenhayn learned that the Kaiser had summoned Hindenburg and Ludendorff. He knew what this meant and resigned. With Hindenburg and Ludendorff taking over the German war effort on all fronts, Falkenhayn was sent to command the German forces in Romania. The mettle of Hindenburg and Ludendorff would soon be tested. Haig was not only going to press ahead with his offensive, but he was going to do so with a new secret weapon.

A French spotter plane flies over a shell-torn no-man's-land in 1916.

The Tank

Two factors gave the Allies hope for their September campaign on the Somme. The first was the arrival of the French 10th Army under General Alfred Micheler to extend the front several miles to the south. The second was the first use of the tank in battle.

The idea of a "landship" had appeared as soon as trench warfare became established. In 1915 the British developed some armored, tracked vehicles (specially designed for crossing trenches), and early the following year the army ordered one hundred of these remarkable new machines. They were

Private Charles Cole remembers how inefficiently tanks were first used:

"Well, we were at the parapets, waiting to go over and waiting for the tank.... The tank never came.... Well, we went over the top and got cut to pieces because the plan had failed. Eventually, the tank got going and went past us. The Germans ran for their lives—couldn't make out what was firing at them.... The tank went on, knocked brick walls, houses down, did what it was supposed to have done—but too late!"

Quoted from Lyn Macdonald, *1914–1918: Voices and Images of the Great War*

formed into the Machine Gun Corps, Heavy Section and nicknamed "tanks" (i.e., water tanks) to help keep their real purpose secret.

Flers-Courcelette

On September 15 Rawlinson's Fourth and Gough's Reserve Armies attacked down the Albert–Bapaume Road, near the villages of Flers and Courcelette. The assault was spearheaded by 37 Mark I tanks, some armed with cannons, others with machine guns. The effect was extraordinary.

In many places the Germans fled in terror before the steel monsters that crunched through wire and lumbered over broad trenches at a steady 3.4 miles (5.5 kilometers) per hour. In one of the most spectacular advances on the Western Front during the entire war, the Allies moved forward more than 2.8 miles (4.5 kilometers). The attack finally relented when the tanks broke down or became bogged in difficult terrain.

Critics say that more machines should have been used in the first tank attack and they should have been better supported. But this assumes what we know now: that tanks (and aircraft) would eventually change the way war was fought. On the Somme, the first tank attack was a gamble that paid off. For all his shortcomings, Haig was not slow to grasp its significance. Shortly after the battle he ordered another one thousand tanks for future campaigns.

Canadian Forces

Troops from Canada played a key role in the Battle of the Somme, but at great cost. The "Byng Boys," commanded by Lieutenant-General Sir Julian Byng, followed the successful tank attack on Courcelette on September 15. In November the Canadians fought with astounding bravery to capture two key enemy trenches. Some 24,029 Canadians were killed or wounded on the Somme, but they earned a reputation as the fiercest of Allied forces.

The Battle Goes On

Flers-Courcelette aside, September was another tough month for the Allies on the Somme. So were October and November. Nevertheless, some progress was made. In late September the British advanced at Morval and the French extended the dent in the German line, but there was no breakthrough. By now, no one was expecting one.

Further north, the fortress village of Thiepval, which had overlooked the British front line for so long, was finally captured on September 27. In October, with the weather deteriorating, Haig concentrated on the high ground before the village of Le Transloy. A few painful gains were made toward the Transloy Ridges.

Mules fight the elements to haul shells through deep mud in November 1916.

Sergeant W.J. Hoyles took part in the Beaumont Hamel attack:

"By the time I got my section up to the top of the hill we were being enfiladed [attacked from the side] by machine-gun fire. We were crouching in a shell-hole, a very shallow one, waiting to go on, and this burst of machine-gun fire took the tops of their heads straight off. I lost the whole of my section—every single man! I got it in the lung, and that was the end for me. The whole thing was an absolute muck-up."

Quoted from Lyn Macdonald, *Somme*

One Last Push

By November 1916 Haig was prepared to call off the battle and start making plans for a new offensive in the spring of 1917. Not so the French. At last they were making notable advances at Verdun, and Joffre insisted that Haig assist his ally by keeping up the pressure on the Somme. The British commander, who liked Joffre and generally got along well with him, agreed to "one last push."

On November 12 General Gough's Fifth (ex-Reserve) Army, which included Highlanders and the Royal Naval Division, took advantage of a break in the weather to make a surprise attack north of the Ancre River. This assault —the last engagement of the First Battle of the Somme—was fought over precisely the same territory as the first day.

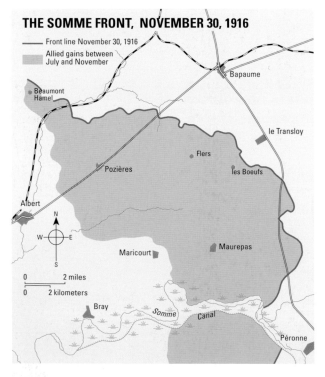

THE SOMME FRONT, NOVEMBER 30, 1916

—— Front line November 30, 1916

Allied gains between July and November

Beaumont Hamel

Bapaume

le Transloy

Flers

Pozières

les Boeufs

Albert

N
W—E
S

Maricourt

Maurepas

0   2 miles
0   2 kilometers

Bray

Somme Canal

Péronne

The attackers were more experienced now. Their bombardments were more concentrated and their troops generally less exposed. There was no question of walking toward enemy trenches, for example. By November 18, the day the offensive was finally halted, the villages of Beaumont Hamel and Beaumont-sur-Ancre had fallen into Allied hands. However, the German line between Serre and Gommecourt farther north remained unbroken. The position of the line was precisely what it was on July 1.

CHAPTER SEVEN

The Second Battle of the Somme, 1918

The year 1917 proved an even more momentous year than 1916 had been. In the east, revolution in Russia brought to power a communist government determined to take the country out of the war. On the Western Front the French Army, close to collapse, became incapable of further offensives. Undaunted, Haig pressed on with his strategy of attrition, this time launching a costly offensive at Ypres (July 31–November 10).

Enter the United States

Perhaps the most important development of the year took place on the other side of the Atlantic. Angered by German attacks on neutral shipping and offers of help to Mexico if it would invade the southern United States, in April 1917 the United States joined the war on the Allied side.

The entry of the United States into the war had little immediate impact on the fighting. The U.S. Army was small and unused to trench warfare. The Germans knew, however, that in time the United States would be able to provide an army larger than that of either Britain or France. If that were allowed to happen, the Central Powers would be doomed. Germany needed immediate victory on the Western Front.

U.S. troops arrive in France in the spring of 1918. It was several more months before such men were ready for the rigors of the Western Front.

U.S. Forces

The American Expeditionary Force (AEF) was commanded by the tough, stern General John Pershing. Visiting Europe in June 1917, he believed it would take three million U.S. soldiers to influence decisively the outcome of the war. Raising and training such a force took a long time and only a few Americans were ready to resist the German spring offensive of 1918. By the end of the war, however, there were two million U.S. troops in Europe, playing an important part in the Allied advance of September–November 1918.

The Spring Offensive

Ludendorff took responsibility for masterminding the planned breakthrough. First, he transferred hundreds of thousands of troops from the east. Second, he chose his tactics: sudden advances by well-trained stormtroopers after a short but intensive bombardment using gas and high explosives. The key to success was speed. The advancing troops were not to worry about what was happening on their flanks, but to drive on relentlessly.

Ludendorff's third decision was his target. He went for a 49.7-mile (80-kilometer) stretch of line held by the undermanned British Third and Fifth Armies. This section of the front ran south from Arras to La Frère. Much of it was very familiar territory—the old Somme battlefield of 1916.

Operation Michael

Ludendorff launched his attack—called "Operation Michael"—on March 21, 1918. Sixty-three German divisions smashed into 26 British, with dramatic effect. Some units resisted to the last. Others, overwhelmed, dispirited, ill-prepared, and ill-led, surrendered or simply ran away. The Second Battle of the Somme was the first time on the Western Front that British troops had been driven back in defeat.

A final, desperate offensive: German stormtroopers attacking during General Ludendorff's spring offensive, 1918.

The Germans kept up the pressure. Over the next three days, Allied tensions grew as the French and British armies were forced apart. Eventually, it was agreed at an emergency top-level conference on March 26 at Doullens, near Amiens, that the French General Ferdinand Foch should be placed in overall Allied command on the Western Front. Even Haig accepted the decision. Without total cooperation, he realized, the Allies would probably lose the war.

Survival

Despite their initial successes, the German advance north of the Somme was halted on March 26, 1918. In the south it surged on toward Amiens before Ludendorff called it off on April 5. His soldiers were utterly exhausted. He had lost over 250,000 men, mostly irreplaceable elite troops. Allied air supremacy had hampered his advance. The effect of an Allied blockade of Germany played its part, too: German soldiers frequently stopped to gorge themselves on captured food and drink rather than continue with the attack.

Captain C.M. Slack recalls the German breakthrough in March 1918:

"We were attached to a Brigade commanded by a man called Haig, a cousin of Douglas Haig— Brigadier Haig—and it was a regular mess up. I retired with the whole of the Fifth Army. By the end of 10 days, the Fifth Army had gone back 50 miles, and we kept doing counterattacks, take that wood, lose it, take it again, and so on. We kept going backwards and forwards, but it was always one step forward and three back, till we got to the other side of the Somme."

Quoted from Lyn Macdonald, *1914-1918: Voices and Images of the Great War*

The "smashed and disfigured terrain" of the old Somme battlefield slowed the German advance in the spring of 1918.

Finally, there was the legacy of 1916. During Operation Michael the Germans pursued the British Third and Fifth Armies across the trenches, craters, and ruins of the old Somme battlefield. The terrain was so smashed, so disfigured, that swift movement was almost impossible. Ironically, therefore, the British failure to advance decisively in 1916 played its part in the Germans' inability to do the same in 1918.

Ludendorff did not give up after Operation Michael. He launched three more offensives. The third crumbled before Foch's counterattack on the Marne on July 18, 1918. The tables were turned and it looked as if Germany might lose the war.

General Erich Ludendorff

Although in theory subordinate to Chief of Staff Hindenburg, from 1916 to almost the end of the war Ludendorff ("the silent dictator") was the dominant figure in the German war effort. He masterminded his country's successful defensive strategy on the Western Front during 1917. In the spring of 1918, however, he gambled—and lost—everything on a swift and sudden victory. His nerve cracked in the fall of 1918 and he resigned. After the war he was influential in the early Nazi party.

For these German troops, surrender was the best option as the German offensive in 1918 lost momentum and Foch began to counterattack.

CHAPTER EIGHT

The Legacy of the Somme

When discussing the Battle of the Somme, the British understandably focus on the first day. This can give a false picture of the campaign as a whole. There was no clear-cut victory, but in military terms it was the Germans, not the British, who suffered the most.

The German Ordeal

The campaign made it most unlikely that Germany would win the war in the West. Before July 1, German forces had dominated on the Eastern Front, advanced almost to Paris, beaten off Allied counterattacks in the West, and gone a considerable way toward "bleeding France white" at Verdun. After the Somme, apart from the final attack in the spring of 1918, the Germans were too battered to do anything but defend.

Germany's losses were a staggering 650,000 casualties (killed or wounded). This was considerably more than the combined total suffered by the French and British. It was also significantly more than those lost at Verdun (434,000), although British accounts of the Somme have sometimes overlooked this fact. Furthermore, as Ludendorff observed, "The strain on physical and moral strength was tremendous." Bombarded day and night, attacked incessantly, harassed from the air, deprived of sleep, driven to living like rats in muddy craters or deep underground in foul-smelling pits—no infantryman could stand being at the battlefront for more than a few days at a time. To keep up morale, the

German prisoners of war arrive in southern England. After the horrors of the Western Front, life in a prisoner of war camp was comparatively comfortable.

forces had continually to be changed. More than half the German Army (95 divisions) served on the Somme at one time or another. Some units returned three or four times.

Strategy and Leadership

The Somme brought the downfall of Falkenhayn and the failure of the German campaign against Verdun. Between January and April 1917, the German Army retired behind the prepared defenses of the Hindenburg Line. Its commanders had accepted that their only hope of victory lay in soaking up pressure, not applying it.

Allied Failings

In his official report on the Somme campaign, Haig played down his aim of breaking through the enemy lines. We now know, however, that this is what he hoped to achieve. Consequently, his Somme offensive was a partial failure.

Defense in depth: This photograph shows a stretch of the almost impregnable Hindenburg Line.

The Hindenburg Line

The Hindenburg Line was a series of defensive positions that ran behind the Somme battlefield from Drecourt to St. Quentin. Sections of the line were named after legendary German heroes, such as Siegfried and Wotan. Started in September 1916 and finished in January 1917, the line comprised an almost insurmountable, deep barrier of barbed wire, trenches, and bunkers. It was not pierced until September 1918, when it was attacked simultaneously by French, British, Belgian, and U.S. troops.

It was a tragedy in terms of losses, too: 419,000 British (14 percent of these on the first day) and 194,450 French. The way so many of these men were lost was also scandalous: ill-planned offensives, failures to follow up gains, inadequate and inaccurate artillery bombardments, and so on. The territorial gains were pitiful. The village of Les Boeufs, the furthest the Allies advanced, was only 6.2 miles (10 kilometers) from their starting point.

Falkenhayn was not the only big-name casualty of the Somme. Allied disappointments helped bring down the British Prime Minister, Herbert Asquith, for whom David Lloyd George took over in December 1916. The French commander-in-chief, Joffre, was replaced by General Robert Nivelle in the same month.

Was he friend or foe? A French infantryman with the skull of an unknown soldier who had been killed and buried in this trench earlier in the war.

The young poet Wilfred Owen (killed on November 4, 1918) wrote this poem after seeing a victim of a gas attack.

... If you could hear, at every jolt, the blood
Come gargling from the froth-corrupted lungs,
Obscene as cancer, bitter as the cud
Of vile, incurable sores on innocent tongues—
My friend, you would not tell with such high zest
To children ardent for some desperate glory,
The old lie: Dulce et decorum est
Pro patria mori.

The Latin in the last line means: "It is sweet and honorable to die for one's country."

The Achievement

For all the disappointments, the Somme campaign brought the Allies substantial benefits. As planned, pressure was taken off the French at Verdun as well as the Russians and the Italians. The German Army had been severely battered and demoralized. The British Army had been battered, too, but its morale remained intact. By the end of 1916, Britain had an experienced, capable, and substantial conscript army for the first time in its history. Lessons had been learned, particularly about the deployment of artillery. Tanks had emerged as a weapon of formidable potential. Most important, the British and French had been forced into closer cooperation.

It is impossible to draw up a simple "profit and loss account" of the Battle of the Somme. Nevertheless, since its consequences were more favorable for them than for their enemies, the Allies could claim a victory of sorts.

Haig never had serious doubts about the validity of the First Battle of the Somme in 1916:

"The enemy's power has not yet been broken, nor is it yet possible to form an estimate of the time the war may last before the objects for which the Allies are fighting have been obtained. But the Somme Battle has placed beyond doubt the ability of the Allies to gain those objects. The German Army is the mainstay of the Central Powers, and a full half of that Army, despite all the advantages of the defensive, supported by the strongest fortifications, suffered defeat on the Somme this year."

Quoted from H.W. Wilson and A.A. Hammerton (eds.), *The Great War*

International cooperation: from left to right, General Joffre, President Raymond Poincaré of France, King George V, General Foch, and Sir Douglas Haig.

*An officer talks to a wounded
private. The Battle of the
Somme fed working-class
people's disillusionment with
Britain's traditional ruling elite.*

Land of Hope and Glory

For Britain, the principal effects of the Somme
campaign were social and political. It was one of the
turning points in modern British history. For a century,
Britain and its people had oozed confidence. They had
boasted the largest empire in history, and their
industrial and commercial prowess had made them the
richest nation on earth. There seemed nothing that the
British—the nation that ruled the waves and lived in a
"land of hope and glory"—could not do. Their self-
confidence was unshakable.

However, even before the outbreak of war, there were
signs that Britain's golden age was starting to fade. Its
wealth was challenged by Americans and Germans. Its
military might was challenged by a handful of South
African rebels in the Second Boer War (1899–1902).
Nevertheless, the real blow came in 1916.

First, in a deeply embarrassing engagement in the North Sea (the Battle of Jutland, May–June), the German Navy outgunned the British fleet. Then came July 1; all those innocent volunteers, the cream of their generation, sacrificed for what seemed no purpose at all. Stories seeped home of the officers' incompetence and, worse still, their callous indifference. From that time on, the nation's confidence in itself and in its leaders began to drain away.

When war threatened in 1878, the Victorians had sung: "We don't want to fight, but, by Jingo!, if we do, We've got the ships, we've got the men, we've got the money too." Forty years later, confidence had turned to cynicism as the men in the trenches sang: "I want to go home, I want to go home, I don't want to go in the trenches no more, Oh my, I don't want to die, I want to go home."

The Somme, more than any other factor, was largely responsible for this change.

Australian soldiers pay their respects to fallen comrades at a cemetery near Albert in the winter of 1916–17.

Timeline

(WF = Western Front)

1905   Schlieffen Plan drawn up.

1907   Anglo-Russian entente.

1914   **July–August** War spreads across Europe.

September 6–16 German advance stopped at the Battle of the Marne (WF).

Falkenhayn replaces von Moltke as German commander-in-chief.

October First Battle of Ypres (to November) (WF).

Turkey joins Central Powers.

December First Battle of Champagne (to March 1915) (WF).

1915   **February** Germany begins unrestricted submarine warfare (to September).

March Battle of Neuve-Chapelle (WF).

April Allies land at Gallipoli but fail to secure a foothold.

Second Battle of Ypres (to May) (WF).

May Italy joins Allies.
Germans make gains on Eastern Front.

Battle of Artois (WF).

August Germans capture Warsaw (Poland).

September Bulgaria joins Central Powers.
Second Battle of Champagne (to October) (WF).

Battle of Artois-Loos (to November) (WF).

December Joffre becomes French commander in chief.

Haig replaces French as British commander in chief.

1916   **February** Falkenhayn begins attack on Verdun (to December) (WF).

May–June Naval Battle of Jutland.

July Russian (Brusilov) offensive on Eastern Front (to September).

July 1 Allied offensive on the Somme (to November 18) (WF).

July 14–September 3 Somme: Battles of Bazentin Ridge, Delville Wood, and Pozières Ridge (WF).

August Romania joins Allies.
Hindenburg replaces Falkenhayn as German commander in chief.

September 3–22 Somme: Battles of Ginchy and Flers-Courcelette (WF).

September 25–28 Somme: Battles of Morval and Thiepval Ridge (WF).

October 1–November 11 Somme: Battles of Transloy Ridges and Ancre Heights (WF).

November 12–18 Somme: Battle of Beaumont Hamel (WF).

December Lloyd George replaces Asquith as British Prime Minister. Joffre replaced by Nivelle as French commander-in-chief.

1917 **January** Germans begin to fall back to Hindenburg Line (WF).

February Germans reintroduce unrestricted submarine warfare.

March Revolution in Russia.

April French offensive (WF).

April 6 United States declares war on Germany.

June First U.S. troops land in France.

July Third Battle of Ypres (to November) (WF).

November Communist revolution in Russia.

1918 **March** Ludendorff launches final German offensive (to July) (WF). Foch appointed supreme Allied commander (WF).

July Allied counterattack begins (WF).

August Allies launch Amiens Offensive (WF).

September Hindenburg Line breached (WF).

November 11 Armistice ends World War I.

Glossary

alliance agreement between states for their mutual help in time of war.

Allies Britain, France, Italy, Russia, the United States, and the countries that fought with them in World War I.

ally a state that has formally agreed to assist another, usually in war.

ANZAC Australia and New Zealand Army Corps.

armistice cease-fire.

artillery heavy guns.

attrition wearing down the enemy.

Austria-Hungary dual monarchy of Austria and Hungary, joined in 1867.

BEF British Expeditionary Force, ready in 1914 to move rapidly to Europe. Later, the term was used for all British forces in France.

blockade cutting off supplies.

blockhouse concrete shelter.

bombardment attack with heavy artillery.

brigade army unit of about one thousand men.

bunker underground shelter, normally made of concrete.

cabinet leading members of the British government.

campaign series of battles.

Central Powers Germany, Austria-Hungary, Turkey, and Bulgaria.

chief of staff top military commander.

communist a person believing in a central government that owns most things and distributes wealth equally among all people.

conference high-level meeting.

conscription obligation by law to join the armed forces. Also called "the draft."

division army unit of about twenty thousand men.

Eastern Front battle front between the Central Powers and Russia.

empire many territories, sometimes in different parts of the world, under the same government.

engagement battle.

entente agreement.

front front line, where two opposing armies meet.

Gallipoli peninsula at the entrance to the Black Sea.

grenadier traditionally, a soldier armed with grenades.

Hindenburg Line German defensive line of barbed wire, trenches, machine-gun posts, and bunkers.

howitzer short-barreled artillery piece that fires at a steep angle.

Kaiser German emperor.

minister person responsible for an area of government, such as war or finance.

morale mood or spirit of a people at war.

mortar metal tube with a firing pin at the bottom that launches a bomb at more than 45 degrees.

munitions ammunition.

offensive large-scale attack.

outflank attack the enemy by moving around the side of their line.

prime minister leading or chief minister, the head of government.

propaganda political information (often false) that gives only one point of view. Like advertising, it is designed to influence the way people think.

Prussia area of eastern Germany around Berlin.

revolution complete, swift, and permanent change—e.g., the overthrow of a government.

Schlieffen Plan German plan for war against France (helped by Britain) and Russia, 1914.

sector part or section.

shrapnel small pieces of metal that fly in all directions when a shell or bomb explodes.

stalemate position where no side appears to be able to win; deadlock.

stormtroopers German infantry unit trained as fast-moving shock troops.

strategy overall war plan.

Territorials part-time British reserve troops set up before World War I.

Western Front front lines between the Allies and the Central Powers in France and Belgium.

Sources and Resources

Further Reading

Dyer, Geoff. *The Missing of the Somme.* New York: Sterling Publishing, 2001.

Keegan, John. *Illustrated Face of Battle.* New York: Viking Penguin, 1999.

MacDonald, Lyn. *To the Last Man: Spring 1918.* New York: Avalon, 1999.

Van Hartesveld, Fred R. *The Battles of the Somme, 1916: Historiography and Annotated Bibliography.* Westport, CT: Greenwood, 1996.

Index